DOWNLOAD THE AUDIOBOOK FREE!

Includes Exclusive Author Commentary

Just to say "Thank You" for purchasing my book, I would like to give you the audiobook version that includes additional examples, stories, and insights to continue bringing the Mindset and Method to life-all for **100% FREE!**

Download at www.iThinkBusiness.Academy

Introduction

Remember when you first started in business and thought, "I wanna' be a business owner so I can make more money and have all the time and freedom I want?" How's that going?

Despite the title, I want you to know I am not suggesting you actually start a franchise. But I do want you to build your business LIKE it's a franchise prototype. Which means utilizing the mindset and method franchise companies use to develop, grow, and scale.

There are groups this book is not for. Those who see their business as their work, as their job. As a way to make a living. This book won't suit those who have already decided they will be closing their business once exhausted from working. It's also not for those who work happily and directly with their customers, continuously earning the satisfaction of a job well done. Content with this pattern until the time to retire arrives. Please know, that nothing is wrong with those scenarios. However, this book will not resonate with you.

If you still believe in your entrepreneurial dreams this book is for you. The four distinct groups it serves are: 1) Those who want to franchise their business; 2) Those who want to open up multiple locations; 3) Family/ legacy businesses handing off from one generation to the next; or 4) Those who want to operate like a franchise prototype so they can truly enjoy the benefits of business ownership. For that is the purpose of a business—to enhance the owner's life by making their entrepreneurial dreams come true with the lifestyle and all the time, money, and freedom they envisioned. The purpose of a business is NOT to suck the life out of you and those around you. Though that is exactly what the vast majority of businesses do. This book will reveal how to escape that.

This project was never part of some grandiose plan. Though life's twists and turns always seem to make the unplanned seem that way. Inspiration for its creation came from three things: a conversation about graphic novels with my daughter Bella, advice from Peter F. Drucker's writings to, "Make Strength Productive", and the following quote—

"The definition of genius is taking the complex and making it simple." –Albert Einstein

The result is a business picture book. One that describes a mindset and method of doing business that reflects my passions. With over 30 years as an entrepreneur, business owner, and student of the craft of business, I offer this book to help minimize the trial and error plaguing those most committed to finding that more direct, less time-consuming/life-sucking path—to success.

The Mindset and Method have been distilled from twelve concepts you will discover herein. While there are hundreds of concepts to learn in business, these twelve must take priority. For they immediately create different actions in your work on a daily and weekly basis. There is a natural order to everything in this world. The endeavor to build a successful business has a natural order as well. And these dozen concepts are the very first twelve one must grasp and understand.

While the simplicity of this book is its strength, the ability to delve further into each concept is its weakness. For it's just a picture book. And can only pique your interest in each concept—can only hope you'll see the exponential power possible when all twelve concepts are packaged together as one whole mindset and method. This book is simply the entrance to that path and if entered, will reveal an exciting world of business you may never have thought existed. The same world I have come to love. One where an individual can take the stage, share their passion, and then lead others to also live, grow, and in turn share within that organization.

Ultimately, this book is a call to those who want to create something bigger than just themselves. It's an alarm—to wake up and consciously begin working and living with the proper mindset toward the goals and dreams you've envisioned. This book serves as a demand to finally take right action. For that is your responsibility. You are the leader of your organization and the one who signed up for the "job" of entrepreneur. I invite you to embrace your responsibility to succeed by moving forward and reading on so you can discover what it takes to build a business that can finally make your entrepreneurial dreams come true. Though this only serves as an abbreviated introduction to the process of building, I hope you gain a new outlook on business, maybe even a new perspective on life.

To Fulfillment and Success,

Marton Medina

Founder, Entrepreneur, and Coach

Dedication and Acknowledgements

Dedicated to my wife.
The müs is loose.

I Want to Thank:

The whole family for your unconditional love and support, especially Ashley, Bella, and Zak for your expertise in making this project look, read, and sound great, and Ty for being the greatest Hype-Man ever.

Tony Faggioli for your rent-a-friend conversations about business and life.

Cornelius Kuncana (Creativius studio), on the other side of the world, for the professionalism and talent you and your illustration team have provided.

The Beta Reader Group who had a marked impact on the shape of this project-Kevin Berson, Alex Cabrera, Zora Chase, Tony Degravina, Jaime Diaz, Tony Faggioli, Kristina Flynn, Rick Grossman, Stephanie Hayes, Bob Helbing, Lisa Johnson, Paolo Ontalan, Michael Pullinger, Bob Scott, Dave Segimoto, Nelly Segimoto, Gene Valdez, and Ben Yap.

Michael E. Gerber for introducing me to the concept of a Franchise Prototype through his book The E-Myth Revisited and whose business owner and coaching programs helped ignite my passion for coaching. His own passion for building "businesses that work" one I share and aim to help carry forward.

The one and only boss I've ever had, who in a 10-month stint as his employee, helped me truly "feel" the importance of entrepreneurship and why one must consciously spend their (life)time doing the work they love.

My clients past and present, whose eagerness to learn, work hard, and commit to the iThink philosophy of business (and life) have validated the Mindset and Method.

And most of all I want to thank God, who gifted me the world of business that has allowed me to know and understand Him better.

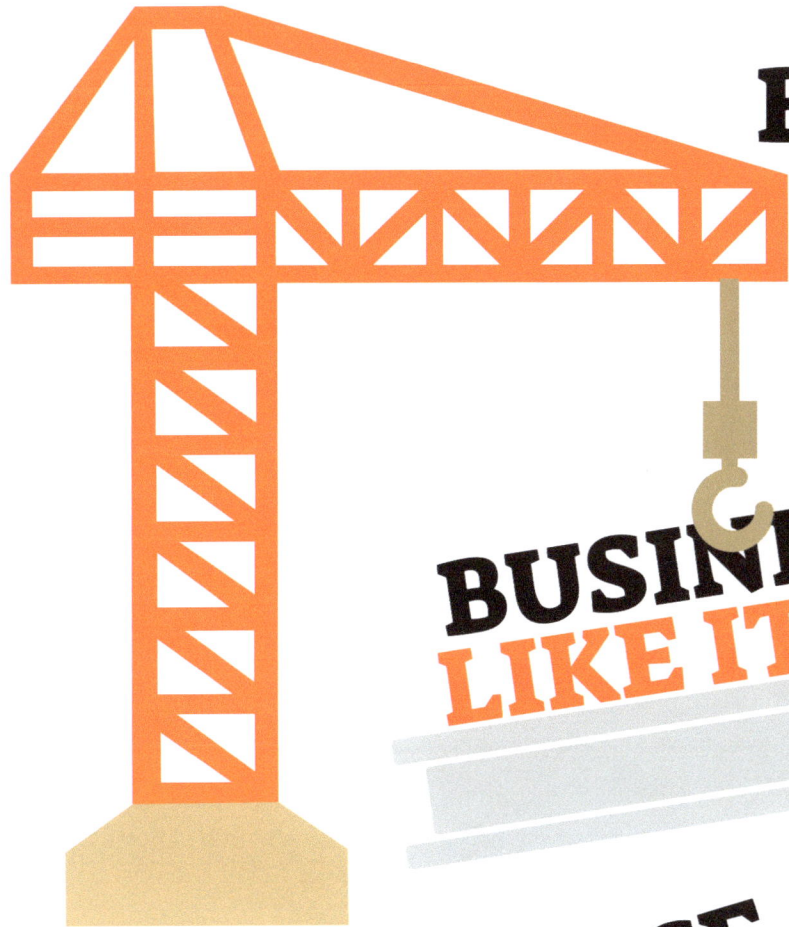

BUILD YOUR

BUSINESS
LIKE IT'S A

FRANCHISE PROTOTYPE

Table of Contents

CHAPTER 1

The Method to the Mindset - Hiding in Plain Sight

Describing the Method in One Word

There's one main thing that differentiates most independently owned businesses from a franchise.

Really, just one main thing — what is it?

SYSTEMS!

Systems are really what a franchise sells. They sell their system of—

MONEY

MARKETING

MANAGEMENT

CUSTOMER SERVICE

HUMAN RESOURCES

and SALES.

Most small business owners don't fully understand the importance of systems so consequently, they don't make it a priority in their work each week. Let me show you why a system is a critical requirement to succeeding through an example—

The driving system in the United States.

That's a Pretty Big System.

233 million drivers BIG!

This brings us to the big question: How do you maintain a safe driving environment for 233 million drivers traveling all across the streets and highways of the United States?

Well, here's how it works...

MONITORING

A police officer waits on the side of the road, watching drivers drive by. When one driver speeds past, the officer races after them—lights glaring, siren blaring, and maybe even instructions on the loudspeaker to, "Pull Over!!!"

Understand what this does to the driver who was pulled over. Imagine what it does to other drivers who see the traffic spectacle.

ENFORCEMENT

You must pay a fine of $575.

On the date and time listed on the citation, the driver presents themselves to a judge where a fine is paid. Failure to show up or pay will result in even steeper consequences like additional penalties or prison time. The judge can even take your driver's license away.

Do you think the monitoring and enforcement was fair to the driver?

I think they're mad they got a ticket. But I'm sure they know they were caught breaking the rules.

Yes! And that brings up the important point of Training. When the rules and regulations of the driving system are understood before driving, the driver can focus on following those rules as trained. Only when rules are unclear, filled with grey areas, or mainly subjective do complaining and conflict come about.

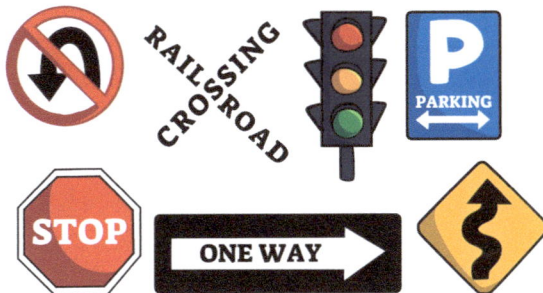

understood

vs.

unclear

Training then...

is where it all STARTS!

You got it! And you can see how clear and precise the training is within the U.S. Driving System. Everyone knows the rules of the road. Drivers don't need the police or a judge to know whether a driving rule is being complied with or broken. ALL drivers can see for themselves whether a fellow driver is following the rules or not. That's how exact the driving system is.

So who's responsible for training the U.S. Driving System?

That's a lot of training!

Sure is! Good thing there's a sub-system called the DMV— the Department of Motor Vehicles.

The DMV is in charge of making sure every driver is properly trained.

All drivers are tested and certified before being issued a Driver's License and given the privilege to drive.

Now, let's pair up this example with our own businesses.

That way we can see how a well-developed system would improve operations. Try plugging in each piece of the example into the different parts of your own business. Beginning with the driver in the U.S. Driving System. Who does that represent in your company?

Yep! I'm beginning to see the connection.

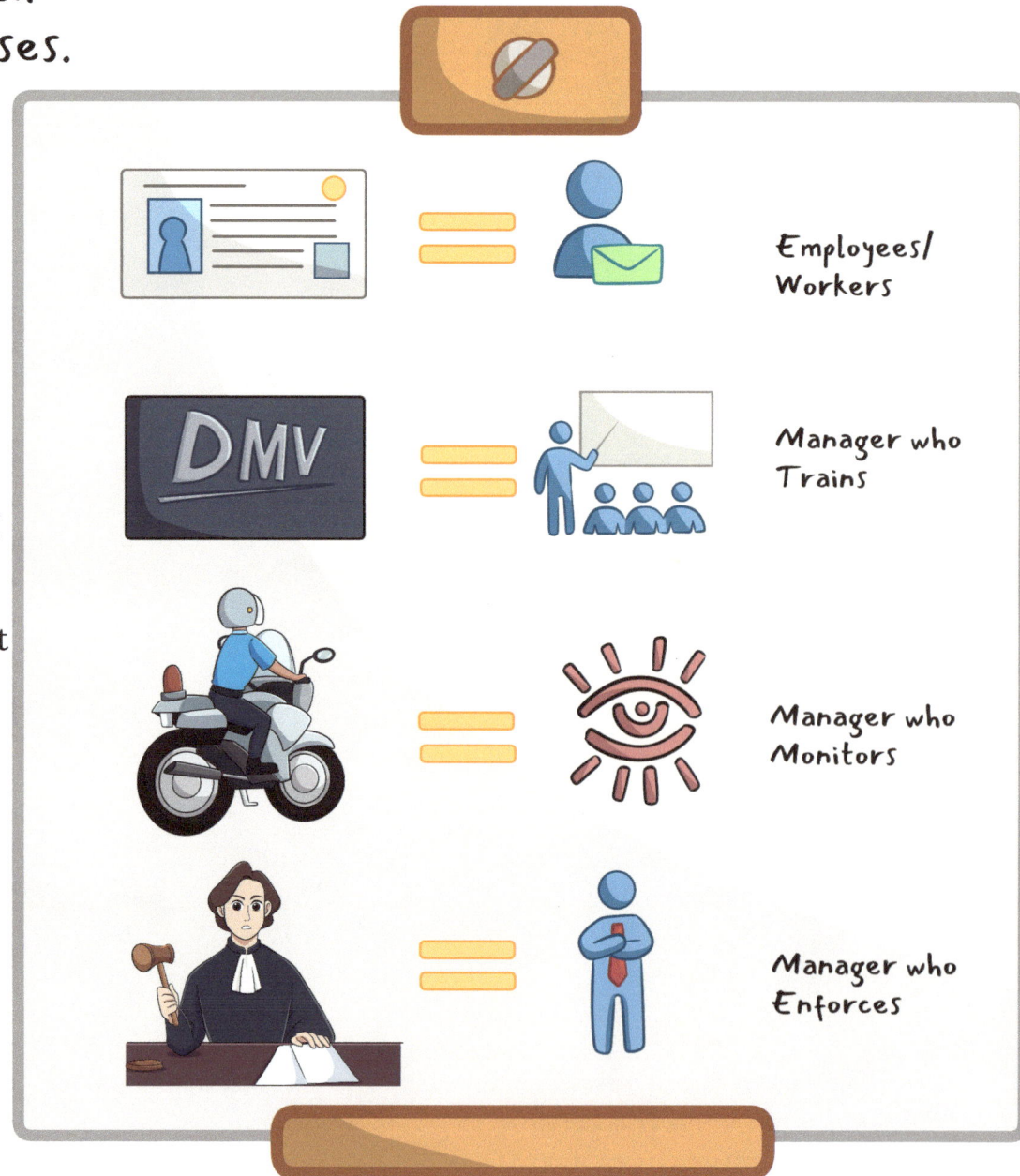

= Employees/ Workers

DMV = Manager who Trains

= Manager who Monitors

= Manager who Enforces

The Method Described in One Word—SYSTEMIZATION

Systems are how you build a business so that work is done "as if" you were doing the work itself. Once a system is properly installed your business immediately becomes less dependent on you. Systems require a "hands-off" approach to doing business which is extremely difficult for owners who have always worked "hands-on" IN their businesses, content to diligently do the work their company was built on. But inside, if you are restless and fighting the idea of settling to just work-work-work your life away, if you are different, with goals and dreams bigger than yourself, then understand—changing from "hands-on" to "hands-off" must be done. To think this way here is the first half of the mantra used to help cue the Franchise Prototype Mindset™ —

Think Like a Big Business...

"Think" is the operative word. I'm not suggesting you BE a big business, have 3,000 employees, or grow to $30 million in sales. Although you can aim for that if you'd like. Instead, I'm asking that you THINK like a big business. Think like your business is a Franchise Prototype preparing to roll out across the country. Adopting this mindset will force you to build and systematize your business while positioned at the helm, not at ocean level where every breaking wave splashes you in the face. You must limit, if not eliminate, your doing of the work itself or services provided to clients and customers. Leave that to the workers—not you. The entrepreneur's focus should be on systemization.

In the next chapter, you will see how this "Big Business" mentality contributes to giving you the proper perspective. This will be important so you can identify and see how some of the most popular beliefs held by business owners, are actually near-sighted barriers keeping you from your entrepreneurial dreams. Once you can see how NOT to think, you'll then be able to understand and complete the other half of the mantra.

Okay. Onward!

CHAPTER 2

Playing Devil's Advocate

Completing the Mantra to the Mindset

PAGE 13

I Know You Are But What Am I?

1. I don't need systems, I trust my people.
2. I don't have time to work on systems.
3. I can do just fine without systems.

With a million things to do each day, thinking about systems is likely NOT on your list. Let's take a deep and devilish dive into why these Top 3 ways of thinking about systems will lead you away from building your business like it's a Franchise Prototype.

I don't need systems, I trust my people.

Maybe you're thinking, "Once I give an employee a responsibility, I trust they will take care of it." Well, imagine using that same logic and *trusting* 233 million drivers across the United States to carry out their driving responsibilities. What would driving in the U.S. look like? What does driving in your company look like?

Face it. What you need first are *systems* you can trust. Then you can work to fill your organization with people you can trust. As you manage your systems, you will see which types of people are a good fit to running your systems well which in turn will tell you who you should be recruiting and hiring. This is the basis of a healthy, exciting, and trustworthy culture.

I don't have time to work on systems.

Of course you don't! And it's pretty obvious where a lot of your time goes instead...fighting fires! Hot ones, explosive ones, as well as the many slow-burning fires that never seem to go out (and never will). All these fires are due to a lack of having the proper systems. So then, how do you work on systems if you're constantly fighting fires? Simple.

Fight Fires _While_ Fighting Fires Anyway.

Okay, that (almost) makes sense — but let me say it differently....

Work ON It _While_ IN It Anyway.

For example, an employee interrupts you for instructions on what to do next. The same situation you're IN 3-4 times every day. As you're explaining what to do, jot some bullet points down (or press record on your phone) as you describe your thinking process, and consequently, come up with the steps you tell them to do.

Use this as training documentation for the situation so when the same thing happens a few hours later, you can refer to it. They can begin solving the problem on their own (with the system you worked ON) without you having to be physically there any longer.

I can do just fine without systems.

You probably never expected systems to be such a major part of your work when starting in business. But as the owner and CEO, you cannot expect your company to operate without well-designed and developed systems. Imagine a large corporation with no systems to guide its hundreds (or thousands) of workers. The company's operations would be chaotic and would implode within weeks.

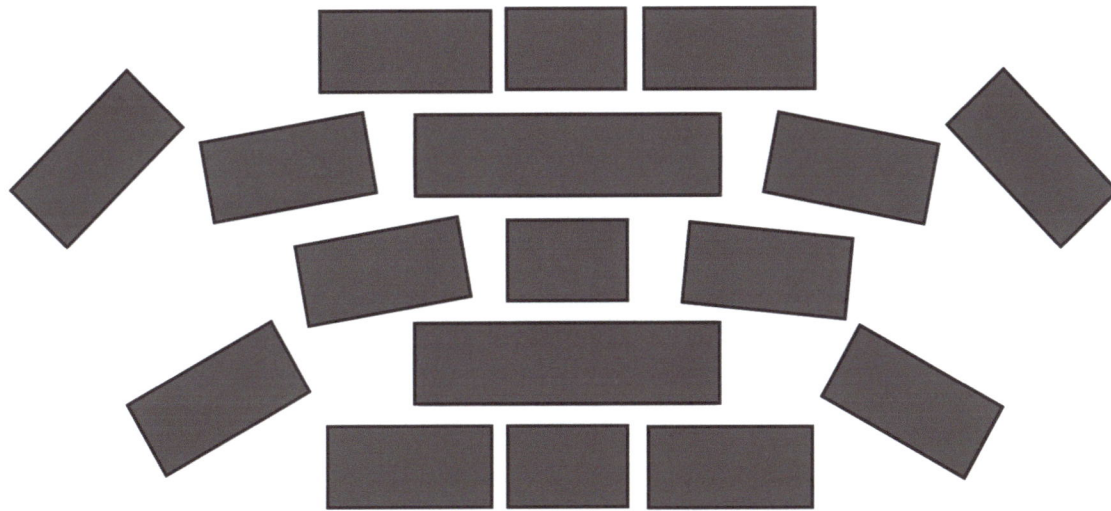

Systems make up the foundation of any business. A lack of systems is the same as a house without a solid foundation. The walls creaking and leaning, held up only by you telling your people to do this and that, all operating upon your command. You are essentially holding up the walls of the house. Your employees leaning on you because there is no foundation of systems to follow otherwise. Feeling like you are running from one room to the other, rotating between walls just before they fall... until you tire. Know, without building a proper foundation of systems exhaustion will eventually set in. And all the walls will fall.

Completing the Mantra to the Mindset

It's interesting to observe opposite ends of the mindset in action. Think like you're building your own Franchise Prototype and you'll begin working on things like image, branding, financial systems, workflow processes, recruiting and hiring standards, and onboarding practices. Think like you alone, **must keep the company afloat** and your priority becomes getting all the work done each day to make sure the customer loves what they've ordered so that you can even receive the "Thank You" yourself. Below is our completed mantra to the mindset that reminds us to think like we're building a Franchise Prototy

"Think Like a Big Business, Not a Micro-Sized Business Owner."

With the benefit of hindsight, you may better see what has been keeping you from making real progress toward your goals and dreams—the fact that you've essentially done zero work on your systems. With that realization and the urge to think like a big business, conscious calls to action will hopefully begin sounding off in your head: "Out of the hundreds of systems I could be working on, what should take priority? Which departments in my business should I work on first, second, and then third? What pattern of work each day and every week will allow me to make progress toward the entrepreneurial vision I want to bring to life?"

If these are the types of thoughts percolating in your mind, know that's a good thing. Time to reach upward by seizing the opportunity only visible to those with the proper mindset. Leave the micro-sized thinking behind and continue to where the work of the true entrepreneur can be found—envisioning, inspiring, and leading all those around.

CHAPTER 3

Rejecting Popular Managerial Myths

Laying the Foundation to Your Management System

PAGE 19

The Top 3 Managerial Myths

REJECTED

1. A manager's job is to manage people.
2. To be a good manager I must work on my management style and personality.
3. Managing people is such a big headache.

Development of the Mindset requires a detour into managerial thinking because systems go hand-in-hand with the managerial position. We'll be debunking a few of the top managerial myths that prevent many from wholeheartedly embracing the genius of systems and the success they create.

Being a professional manager is one of the most fulfilling positions and careers in the workplace. Unfortunately, many don't see it that way, especially since real-world experiences under managers who were not well educated and/or trained far outnumber those ideal managerial experiences where the worker gained a deep sense of fulfillment and satisfaction. The best and most effective managers are those who genuinely care about success—both for their companies and for those who work under them. These three managerial myths help point us to the very heart of managerial success. As we explore the truths behind them you may begin to see what your organization can truly become.

A manager's job is to manage people.

Managing your business may be very different than what you think *managing* is. As Michael E. Gerber, author of The E-Myth Revisited says, "Successful managers DO NOT manage people—they manage *systems*."

Sorry Bud, you haven't hit a ball in the past six months. You know that means I gotta' take you out of the starting lineup.

Systems used by baseball managers show which players hit, catch, and run well. Along with which players don't. Their systems are transparent and exact for all to see. Managers, fans, and the players themselves know how each player is performing. All managers are in charge of making managerial decisions based on what their company's system requires. In the baseball scenario above, the system requires players get at least one hit every six months. Otherwise, they will lose their starting position and get demoted to cheering the team on—from the bench.

To be a good manager I must work on my management style and personality.

Being "nice" is not what is required to be a good manager. Nor is being hard-nosed and tough. Good managers are defined as effective managers which means, as author Peter F. Drucker titled his book, *Managing for Results*. The results each company or organization charges their managers with should be clearly described by the company or organization they lead. Important to note, if you are nice continue being nice. But personality traits like being nice, mean, funny, or approachable have nothing to do with whether a manager is effective or not. Below are a handful of leaders recognized by many as extremely effective managers. As you can see, there is no one winning personality trait or management style. There is only effectiveness and results.

Elon Musk

Confrontational and sometimes erratic behavior. A management style described as management by chaos.

Forbes
by Sally Percy
Sept. 26, 2023

Queen Elizabeth

Reserved, calm, poised, and adaptable.

PBS.org
By Vikram
Mansharamani
Sept. 10, 2015

Abraham Lincoln

Accessible, persuasive, democratic, innovative, and a good storyteller.

TIME
By Eric Barker
Mar. 25, 2014

Steve Jobs

Autocratic, "My way or the highway", charismatic, abrasive, and curious.

Inc.
By Moreal
Schwantes, Inc.
Nov. 22, 2022

Managing people is such a big headache.

Managers are the leaders of human interactions and relationships within their companies. Their impact, whether good or bad, will be felt by every worker around them, making this position one that can be naturally fulfilling. The problem is, most managerial jobs were not designed to use the greatest working relationship tool known to managers—Positive Reinforcement.

You did it! You ran things exactly the way the system was designed. Way to go! I'm so proud of you!!!

Thanks! I can't believe someone even noticed.

And because it's not used enough, most managers are usually seen as cold and heartless. Which in turn leads to divisive rather than productive working relationships. In contrast, when a management system is designed with Positive Reinforcement at its core, magic happens—fulfillment and success become the continuous beating heart of your company's culture.

Laying the Foundation to Your Management System

By rejecting the Top 3 Managerial Myths, three truths are revealed. Successful managers must manage systems, manage for results, and use systems to positively reinforce.

What Your Management System Means

1. To Individuals

Individuals inherently yearn to find achievement and fulfillment in the work they love.

2. As Organizations

Organizations create purpose and cause, and are the means to people working together.

3. For Work

Working in an organization provides access to relationships and community.

Building on the Rock of Truth, Not on Mythical Sands

Business operations built on managing people, personalities, and subjective praise are chaotic and opposite those built on systems, results, and positive reinforcement which nurture good human relations and interactions. Which do you want your people to work within? Which do you want to build and manage?

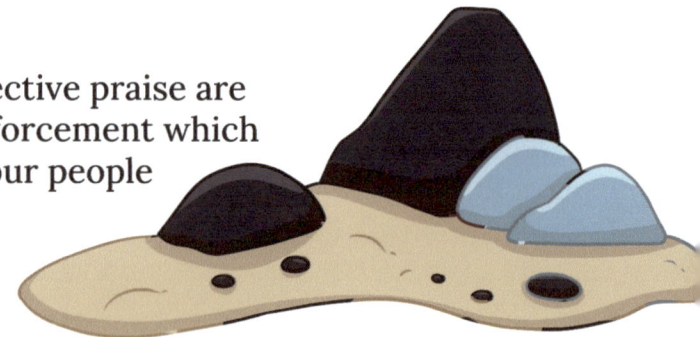

CHAPTER 4

How I Think >
My Circumstances

*It All Begins With Me,
and the Way I Think*

PAGE 25

Mastering One's Craft

It is common to hear business owners complaining about this and that and citing the reasons for their problems as due to the…

Employees or **Customers** or **Economy** or **Area I'm In**

or some other reason outside of themselves. Business owners play a much bigger part in what results they reap. In other words, if you have an employee problem, the reality is it's because you don't know enough about employees and need further development to become a better manager. In contrast, many think their employee problems cannot be solved. And say things like, "I can't help it, I've done all I can, it is what it is. That's employees for you—can't work with 'em, can't work without 'em."

If you have money problems, the reality is it's because your thinking on money is wrong. Instead many believe their difficulties with money are because, "Money is difficult and complex, and I'm not an accountant. And I heard I can skip all this anyway by just increasing sales. They say you can't go wrong with lots of sales."

If you have customer problems, the reality is it's because you don't know enough about client fulfillment, consumer behavior, and how to set up, create, and deliver to customer expectations.

If you're feeling trapped in your business and can't get away, can't get a decent vacation, the reality is you don't know enough about organizational structure and strategy, recruiting and hiring, and all the things that can actually free you up.

Business author and researcher Jim Collins succinctly says, "Greatness is not a result of circumstance but of choice." You may start seeing the vision behind iThink Business Academy or at least the reason for the name. It's an extension of its philosophy and contributes to the idea that asks, "What can *I* do about my employees? What can *I* do about my customers, and my money, or being trapped in my business?

To reach true success, you must take the first step of properly embracing your role as a business owner. And doing that starts with a good, hard look at oneself and understanding, "Yes, of course, I can take credit for the successes within my business. However, I am also responsible for its troubles and failures.

It all begins with me, and the way I think.

How you think is how you'll act. How you act will largely dictate your results. Those results will impact your life, be it positive or negative. Understand that the part of the equation you control wholly is how you think. At this critical juncture see the responsibilities, jobs, and tasks of a business owner as a craft. So you can aspire to be a Master Craftsman (Business Owner), ready to face the realities of business head-on rather than as a result of your circumstances

You are not dictated by your circumstances. Furthermore, it's painful to hear how one's circumstances are the root of their problems. Those moments are like watching someone choke and murder their own entrepreneurial life. This thinking continues to cause a fair share of breathless and unconscious business behavior. You must sharpen your knowledge so you can pierce through the plethora of aimless thinking and mindless excuses. Wake up! Use the Mindset and Method to free yourself from the shackles of circumstance and instead, empower yourself with more life, love, and laughs.

"As iron sharpens iron, so one person sharpens another." —King Solomon, Proverbs 27:17

The purpose of a business is in fact to make all your entrepreneurial dreams come true—not to suck the life out of you *and* those around you.

Ultimately, the hope is for as many as possible to live happily in the world of business making the most of the short, irreplaceable time here on this earth. Pursuing, sharing, and truly living a life well-lived.

CHAPTER 5

Marking the Moment: The Entrepreneurial Time Crux

Taking Control of the Sands of Time

The Entrepreneurial Time Crux

Now that you see how this mindset single-handedly changes the game, it is important to guide you into the next phase of success. This final concept dictates whether or not change will happen for you because the process of transformation requires two parts. The mental change and the actionable change. Your choice to build your business with systems must immediately be followed by action. Otherwise, just like a New Year's resolution without it, nothing will result. The next immediate challenge then—

What to Spend Your Time On

You may immediately recognize how this difficult and important decision will continuously press you. The same dilemma repeats itself every morning when you wake, "There's so much to do...what should I do today?" This truly is the crux of the matter. The critical decision every entrepreneur must make every working day. What will you spend your *time* on to transform your business? This is the Entrepreneurial Time Crux.

Please date and time-stamp this exact moment to mark your initial face-to-face meeting with the Entrepreneurial Time Crux (ETX).

Your ETX Moment:

____ /____ /____ – ____ : ____ am/pm

This initial ETX Moment is the most significant and consequential of them all. It issues you an ultimatum to decide whether to use systemization to build your business. To help you gain clarity of the moment the graphic on the next page reiterates the most important concepts and combines them in a cohesive direction toward the ultimate business goal—

TO BUILD A BUSINESS THAT BRINGS YOUR ENTREPRENEURIAL VISION TO LIFE

"Think Like a Big Business"

What to Spend Your Time On

ENTREPRENEURIAL TIME CRUX

Past Business Owner Experience

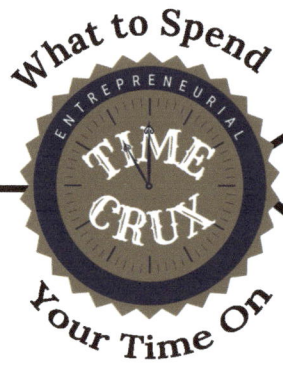

Sharpening Your Tools

Working | Life Event 1 | Life Event 2 | Life Event 3 | Working | Life Event 4 | Life Event 5 | Life Event 6

Systemization

Leverages your efforts to create more time, money, and freedom so you can focus on living a life well-lived.

Status Quo

Based on holding the business up yourself and working-working-working your life away. Maximizes trial and error.

Non-Systemization

Working | Working | Working | Life Event 1 | Working | Working | Working | Life Event 2

"Think Like a Micro-Sized Business Owner"

Know that change will not happen until you decide to take action. If too deeply rooted in the status quo, use your ETX Moment as a measure of inaction and push yourself harder to adopt the Mindset of building your business like it's a Franchise Prototype and "thinking like a big business". Visualize the benefits of systemization as a means of motivation for the time, money, and freedom you crave. Do this over and over again until you are wholeheartedly able to take action. Unless of course, time is not an issue for you, and *later* will suffice. In the meantime, I suspect that you, just like everyone in this world, are running out of time.

Your business.
Your life.
The sands of time
are in your hands.

Redirect the future sands of time you still control. Choose this new direction of thinking that allows you to hope and dream like you once did when you first became an entrepreneur. Choose systemization for your business and your life. Then, take action—for your life's sake, take action!

"He that would perfect his work must first sharpen his tools."
—Confucius

If you've decided to build your business like it's a Franchise Prototype you must first commit, not to building the business, but to building your business *toolbox* and sharpening the entrepreneurial tools required to succeed.

Entrepreneurial Leadership — **Executive Time Management** — **Productivity Planning** — **Prioritization** — **Systemization**

Sharpen these tools in this exact order for when properly ordered and aligned together, they allow you to design and develop those systems crucial to your unique business situation. As each foundational system is set, you can then begin training, monitoring, enforcing, and positively reinforcing. Also, know the pitfalls of being stuck as a micro-sized business owner so you can prevent from falling and losing yourself deep within the endless rabbit holes filled with business owners running on hamster wheels, working-working-working their lives away.

Lastly, learn these things from the best so you are adept at recognizing between right and wrong-way thinking. Then ask yourself, "What else can I do?" And again, "What else can I do *next*?" Until by habit, you are perpetually learning, growing, and developing into a master of the craft of business, a master of your fate, and a true entrepreneurial believer in destiny.

34

Don't forget to download the FREE audio version for exclusive additional author commentary that brings the Mindset and Method to life.

Download at www.iThinkBusiness.Academy

www.ingramcontent.com/pod-product-compliance
Lightning Source LLC
Chambersburg PA
CBHW041750190326

41458CB00031B/6508